Statements Made
in Passing

Kathleen Serley

WATER'S EDGE PRESS
SHEBOYGAN, WI

Printed in the United States of America

Water's Edge Press LLC
Sheboygan, WI
watersedgepress.com

ISBN: 978-1-952526-11-4

Credits

Cover design by Water's Edge Press
Image licensed through iStock

A WATER'S EDGE PRESS FIRST EDITION

Acknowledgements

The author is grateful to the editors of the following publications in which these poems first appeared, some in different form:

Verse and Vision, 2012: "Statements Made in Passing"

Wisconsin Poets' Calendar, 2014: "On her way"

An Ariel Anthology, 2015: "This Silent Night"

Solitary Plover, Summer 2015: "Released from a pocket"

The Clearing Speaks (exhibit), 2015: "Statements Made in Passing"

An Ariel Anthology, 2016: "Peach Time"

Red Cedar, 2016: "My Mother's Will"

Peninsula Pulse, 2018: "Reading Zane Grey"

Solitary Plover, Summer 2018: "Winning"

Trace, 2018: "Highway 40 feels the same"

Centennial Poetry Competition UW-Eau Claire, 2018: "Skipping"

Museletter, Summer 2019: "A Walk in the Woods"

bramble, Winter 2019: "All summer we waited for the melon to ripen"

bramble, Winter 2020: "A Spring Elegy"

Halfway to the North Pole Door County in Poetry, 2020: "Statements Made in Passing"

Wisconsin Poets' Calendar, 2020: "Highway 40 Feels the Same"

Your Daily Poem, March, 21, 2021: "I need brown"

bramble, Summer 2021: "Godspeed: Emails from my Garden"

Barstow & Grand, 2021: "Turning"

Wisconsin Poets' Calendar, 2022: "Salubrity"

To The Garden

Reading Zane Grey 1
A Spring Elegy 2
Summer Rain 3
Tending to the Harvest 4
Someday 5
All summer we waited for the melon to ripen 6
Peach Time 7
Turning 8
Forty years makes a difference 9
Godspeed: Emails from my Garden 10
My Place 12
Statements Made in Passing 13

In The Woods

A Walk in the Woods 17
To Plant a Trillion Trees 18
To the Weeping Willow: an Ode 20
Ode to the Great White Pine in my Backyard 21
The Transplant 22
Untitled 23
Stepping back 24

BY THE WINDOW

Looking out...29

Snowbound...30

This Silent Night..31

Valentine's Day at the Bistro..............................32

Pulled from a Pocket..33

An early spring rain is coating my drive..........34

I need brown..35

Monarch...36

Released from a pocket...37

AT THE DOOR

The traveler..41

Salubrity..42

Three of Cups...43

To the Women of the House................................44

Winning...45

Diary: *March 2020*...**46**

Humble Days..47

To Gustava Pedersdatter of Molthrov...............48

On her way..49

My Mother's Will...50

Highway 40 feels the same..................................51

Skipping..52

To The Garden

Reading Zane Grey

The morning my mother discovered me reading
Zane Grey I learned her secret.
A horse ranch, she said, *I always wanted*
to work on a horse ranch.
She didn't say own.
My mother sold her horse for college.
She didn't aspire to ownership,
just one sure-footed climb up a rocky cliff.
We lived on a city lot, a dozen steps
in full stride to the edge of the drive
but my mother was always pushing
our boundaries. She worked,
for one thing, at a career that had cost
a horse, at a time when most women paced
their city lots. That's what I liked about reading
Zane Grey. The women. How they end up
on a sagebrush flat but manage
to find their way. My mother
was like that even without her horse.

A Spring Elegy

"If we do not permit the earth to produce beauty and joy,
it will in the end not produce food, either."

Joseph Wood Krutch

We walked from her house, along a winding woods road
to a one-lane bridge spanning a swollen trout stream
She had invited me. *Wait 'til you see,* she said,
you won't believe how beautiful

My grandmother seeking beauty surprised me
Each spring she planted a few pansies under an old pine tree,
but hers was a world of faded house dresses and farm chores
I didn't fancy her walking a mile for a view from this bridge

All around us, the land played with color
Orange and lavender in broad strokes
stippled purple and pink. Pastels framed
in a sketch of American cherry fully bloomed

We called each flower by name,
spring beauty, marsh marigold, trillium and trout lily
Tie-dye creations flung to the far corners of the woods
A rainbow upended spilling treasure at our feet

In time, spring blooms gave way to summer grasses and
the land was put to use. Naive to what higher purpose
the land might serve, I longed for another spring
when driven by memory, I scouted the bridge

Below me, the muddied stream lay stilled
beside its trampled banks. Not one flower bloomed
Pastured cows wandered in a dogged quest for grazing,
as, pummeled, the ground gave up its seed

2

Summer Rain

Just when we think Earth has abandoned us, she sends a
summer rain whispering like a drummer's brush held with a
steady hand   *pit-patter pit-patter pit-patter*   a gazillion
droplets shimmering in free fall   *pit-patter pit-patter pit-
patter*   the soil softens in acceptance releasing musk to
scent the air   we settle   watch rain sheets wrap the yard
for a time there is nothing but rain   rain pooling in sunken
corners of the patio   rain kicking up mist beside the road
the hydrangea spreads heart-shaped leaves and we
abandon ourselves   swaying with the steady drumbeat
pit-patter pit-patter pit-patter   tomorrow paper wasps will
take up their work under the eaves, the carrots will need
thinning and flowers in the border will continue their tussle
with the weeds but   Now   a moist breeze reaches through
the window holding out promise

aglitter at dawn
raindrops linger on lilies
gift of summer rain

Tending to the Harvest

Acorns pelt my neighbor's deck like corn popping
all week   lulled asleep   nudged awake   I listen to this
promise of an ample harvest   pledged in early spring when
winds tousled white oak blossoms unseen a hundred feet
above my head   as my father-in law once brushed his
worn hand against tomato vines budding in the garden
snapping a stiff finger to sway the blooms   ensuring, he
said a plentiful harvest   a fancy we thought   a quirk of
fate   his bountiful tomato crop   then I read about those
blooms   how they need to be swayed to release pollen
something bumblebees are good at   vibrating their fuzzy
bodies to shake loose the yellow dust   setting on fruits
aplenty   still, I hear of a light apple crop in fall   of pear
trees barren and pumpkins rotting in flooded fields
inevitable some say   others say a fluke   in my garden,
I cup my hand around a cluster of late tomato buds
set them pulsing   all the while I listen to the steady drop
of acorns skipping off my neighbor's deck

grey squirrels busy
as bees bring in the harvest
bare caps left behind

Someday

Someday there will be rattlesnakes in my rock garden sunning
themselves among the sedum, the creeping phlox
Someday I won't see them staking claim to my backyard
I will bring my hoe, my pruning shears to the garden
my sun hat shading my eyes and there they'll be
looking like any other rock

But not today. Today I will meet a friend for lunch
We'll sit across from each other talk of ordinary things
like this was any other day and not our first time
since Covid corralled us kept us indoors at arm's
length waiting for that unexpected strike

I need to walk in the woods follow a deer trail
through the hemlocks along the river until it opens
on the sunny patch behind my house. I am weary
of groomed trails of suiting up against a threat I can't see
ticks waiting in the willows shed by mice unchecked

I scan the sky looking for a hawk hope for help out of this place
we won't see as unseasonable heat wilts the plants warms
the rocks in my garden where someday there will be rattlesnakes
But not today. Today I will go to the garden bend down
to seek strawberries from among their wide green leaves
as all around me trees breathe in breathe out unseen

All summer we waited for the melon to ripen

cradled in the soft ground its girth swelling
in summer's high heat the melon grew
with the lengthening days stretching
from inches to feet darkening from jade
to emerald green with the tasseling of the corn

we thumped it, ran our summer-browned hands
along its smooth cool sides studied
it while we thinned the carrots shelled the peas
dug new potatoes from their ever-widening hills

the melon stopped growing yet its vine meandered
winding through the corn trailing along the fence, restless
nights cooled, still we waited pulled the last of the carrots
gathered corn stalks into sheaves
the melon left beached in garden sand

we ran short of waiting Dad pulled his
pearl-handled knife from the front pocket
of his overalls rolled the melon a quarter turn
to carve a diamond-shaped plug from its underside

we peered into the depths of our melon
past the tough outer skin beyond
the translucent inner rind to fibers glistening
with a garnet's blush, our wait ripened
to the dream that warm September day

Peach Time

I wish we could have met for lunch today
I would have told you about the peach truck
the cache of golden peaches
I lugged like a miser to my car.
I would have said, let's make a pie
some marmalade and you would have agreed
relishing as always the peach harvest.

Is it enough that I skip my lunch hour
stand in line clutching a wad of moist dollars
waiting in this treeless vacant lot to snag
a box of Colorado peaches from a refrigerator truck.

I won't can them. I lack your energy for peaches.
Instead I will carry them around my neighborhood
offering them in sixes and eights saying,
my mother loved peach time.

Turning

in one loosely sprung coil the apple releases its peel turning in
my cupped hand to the steady scrape of the paring knife garnet-
red swirls settle against the scrubbed whiteness of my kitchen
sink   this is the last of them apples picked in autumn saved over
these many weeks for one more late-winter pie   on the counter
small jars of nutmeg cinnamon and clove wait like a wise man's gift
their mingled scents calling up visions of the little boy snatching
slices before I can seal the crusts the teenager snagging that second
piece on his way out the door   a careful turn and the smooth
dough unwraps from my rolling pin drapes the mounded fruit and
I recall the year I froze my apples   peeled cored and sliced they
waited   I waited   then one blustery March morning he walked
into my kitchen after fifteen months away his eyes wide on reset
from Iraq the smell of apple pie baking working its magic   almost
finished I move the pie plate a quarter turn crimping the edge
as my mother taught me   taking my time   taking my turn

Forty years makes a difference

A nylon mesh tube with room
    for twelve or more restyles your Mason jar
        each release heralded, a stand alone in my yard
            where dozens once blanketed your flower garden

Still that iridescent chrysalis
    hangs suspended by a single thread
        a slight vibration signals the grand escape
            with bold unfolding of those iconic wings

That first princely step along my open hand
    your spirit stretched across generations guiding
        my grandsons' reach with wonder for the monarch
            forty years makes a difference, or no difference at all.

Godspeed: Emails from my Garden

Helen,
Birds are back!
Wren wakes me before dawn
Catbird calls me to the garden
After the long winter, I love these
useful days. . . .
To life, my friend,
K

Lydia,
Berries sugaring on the counter,
this morning's pick. Think
shortcake—the Fourth and
fireworks. Looking forward to
family,
K

Lydia,
The Gentle Shepherd bloomed today—finally
ivory petals opened to a golden throat
An unassuming lily—yet long awaited
When you come home, I'll send a cutting
back with you - every garden needs a
gentle shepherd.
Love,
K

Helen,
Kids here for long weekend. Boys
growing fast, excited for school
to start. L says half their classmates
will get free lunch this year. We must
do more than love our own, my friend.
We must do more.
K

Lydia,
Put in fall bulbs this morning
Remembrance, my favorite purple crocus
A hundred reasons to want for spring
Recalling your summer visit, our walks
together in the garden, so sending this
soft reminder—plant your own fall bulbs
to bloom in spring.
K

Helen,
Made my annual trip to the apple orchard
today thinking all the way of other falls, of
family. Kids climbing high, reaching for the
perfect apple, tugging a loaded wagon over
bumpy ground, sun warm on our backs.
Climbing not allowed in orchard these days.
Still— Happy times, my friend,
K

Lydia,
Made my annual trip to the apple orchard
today—beautiful drive. Wealthy, Cortland,
Macs—a trunkful—too many, I suppose,
yet not near enough. Thinking of apple pies
and crisps, mulled cider for the holidays,
cinnamon and clove. Wishing you home,
K

Helen,
Cold today. Thinking of summer—tomatoes
setting on in the garden—bees busy in the
beans. The promise of way too much
zucchini. Pulled vegetable soup from
the freezer for lunch. Filled me up.
Here's to health, my friend,
K

My Place

My grandmother sewed a butterfly quilt cut
from my school dresses threads worn thin
their best parts becoming red-plaid-pink-flowered
butterflies stitched to muslin squares connected
a coverlet I carried from place to place
I planted gardens roses at first with delphinium
bent by the weight of their purple blooms
but then I planted red milkweed rosy blossoms
standing tall on sturdy stems   I planted
Joe Pye Weed waving lavender plumes and
drifts of goldenrod to remind me of my first
place a field turning yellow in late August
and monarchs hundreds of them truly
blanketing the golden blooms   In my second
place I planted a flowering crab a twig
barely reaching to my shoulder by the time
I had to leave and in my third place I left
a quiet daylily planted for its name
the Gentle Shepherd   I drove past my second place
a pink and white canopy filled the side yard
when I thought *who* and remembered the twig
My grandmother liked butterflies even knew
their names but she didn't pay them much mind
they were always in the alfalfa field fluttering
over plantings near the porch   In this new place
I folded the butterfly quilt tucked it in the blanket
chest to spare it further wear but then I planted
coneflowers a monarch settled on a sturdy bloom

Statements Made in Passing

Gray on gray, fragments of forgotten boulders,
fill miles of deserted shore,
a beach where tumbled stones inhibit strolling, so
I seem alone except for water and the wind-bowed trees.
Yet, ahead of me seven wave cut rocks
stacked square on circle and balanced by design
rise from the thousands similar. A statement made in passing.
I ponder what to add; move on at first then turn,
bend, wrap my hand around a wind-rubbed,
sun-warmed rock too heavy for skipping
and set it atop those already placed, lengthening
the sculpture's shadow slightly
as the great lake pulses, tuned to rhythms of its own.

IN THE WOODS

A Walk in the Woods

I remember walking in the woods with you
and coming upon the mother bear with her twins
a porcupine climbing high
the tree swaying under his prickly weight

I remember the opening in the forest
the immigrant's empty cabin
his yard a carpet of violets
a wild apple tree in full bloom

I remember the fall we made apple jelly
on a stolen day, the filled jars aglow
like a captured September sun

Remember when we hung trail signs named
for your ninjas, the Michelangelo loop
Donatello's straight stretch through the heart of the woods

I will remember this day, walking in the woods
with your sons, the forest cut-over the big trees gone
We looked for seedling oaks four leaves, eight leaves, ten
When they finally form a canopy, remember.

To Plant a Trillion Trees

in response to the "One Trillion Tree Initiative"

I see three white pine clustered in my backyard
a dozen pin oak line my street
but a trillion trees   one million million

picture that

trees stacked like dollar bills
a quarter of the way to the moon
one hundred-fifty trees each   a half acre
planted by every one of us   today

are you game

I'm growing aspen   five thousand sprouts per acre
thirty-five acres   a good start on a trillion trees
but I worry   to save us trees need time
forty years for starters

can we wait

while six inch seedlings do our job
the immigrant here before me chose
to live among his trees   a diverse forest
basswood, hemlock, tall red oak

the great trees felled upon his death
their value couched in dollars bills

18

that's the problem   what we choose

the land came to me cut over
I've held it forty years   a steady steward
waiting for aspen to gain a foothold
for red oak to regenerate

trees take time

to plant a trillion trees we'd best start   today
that's the blessing   we can choose

To the Weeping Willow: an Ode

With branches dipping downward you defy
tradition sending pliant boughs to brush
the ground as trees nearby comply with code
and stretch their branches skyward. You instead
mirror the river bending light through leaves
as water shapes the sun. Asway, your fronds
cascade in quivering arches, a grounded falls
at river's edge, and I recall the ease
of slipping through that tented foliage
the peace secured when rustling amber fans
curtained a space for me to settle screened
from view. Thus sheltered, I observed a grace
in willowy response to shifting drafts,
the play in patterns yielding to change.

Ode to the Great White Pine in my Backyard

Unguarded, taller than the sun you stand
yet anchored to the earth's warm core.
Your canopy afloat like silken scarves
a wave, a swell, a crest in open air.
Descendent of historic forests, named
the tree of peace in ancient lore, you rise
to shelter me through stressful days. Your boughs
in lilting whispers quiet anxious thoughts
as sun-warmed needles settling soft
invite my rest. So I will bury fear
beside the arc of your entwining roots
and sink all sorrows deep in cleansing soil;
aware the winds will free your pollen dust
to turn all wavering shadows gold in time.

The Transplant

with a nod to the Chippewa Valley's Champagne Apple

Apples Ahead beckons at every
bend in this rutted road
coax me deeper into the
darkening wood tempt me with
ever-changing light to venture
far from home tracking a
golden apple a transplant
heralded as the survivor of an
inhospitable clime car window a-
jar to catch the breeze I keep going
keen to find that apple subject of a
likely myth one wild apple grown to
many in a new home as my
Norwegian kin settled here I an
off-shoot one of many sinking roots in a
promised land
questing after an apple
rumored golden just ahead or
so it's said   my kin gave up fjords
trusting stories replete with dreams of
untold treasure waiting in this river
valley's rolling hills welcomed then as
we welcome now the transplant
exchanging one land for another we
yield to change forever
zealous in our search for home

Untitled

I.

Corn stubble stands crisp and still against the hillside
November's pale sun nuzzles the stalks   finds them wanting
spreads out over the groomed ground looking for a way in

II.

Still, crisp corn stubble stands against the hillside
unresponsive to the flirting sun   April rains tease the ground
when will hope take root

III.

Against the hillside, leggy stalks stand in crisp green rows
a high-beamed sun ogles these plants
its hot advances deflected by an indifferent ground

IV.

Corn stubble stands crisp and still against the hillside
bent to trifle with the sun's approach
a black cat picks its way over the frozen field

Stepping back

The broom waits where I left it
leaning against the rain barrel

dried leaves back into corners
pollen dust coats window ledges

I have been away too long, seeking
connection with Norway, a land of hard

surfaces swept clean by glacier ice
and emigration. One million in a century

of leaving, my grandfather two of his three
brothers included. Makes me wonder

about roots, the way they're said to hold
a thing in place, tether it to one spot.

Yet give roots half a chance
and they'll split a rock wide open,

work a hairline crack until a solid
boulder gives way to sand.

I imagine roots had a lot to do with it,
the clean sweep, I mean. They just gave

way, which is why I've not placed
them—set in stone. Roots

would rather stretch out, reaching
for a richness yet untapped

like those three brothers, new growth
grounded by their travels.

Home at last, I reach for my broom.
Sand has gathered along the drive.

BY THE WINDOW

Looking out

Snow drifts across the drive, mounds below the window
settles on pine boughs bent low to brush the window

Too deep, too chill, snow mutes even the jay's shrill call
a hush seeps, like something borrowed, through the window

Not always so, a quiet day brought low by snow
once boys laughed to see it billow near the window

We filled the time with projects saved, with games and song
all tucked in   plump bread dough resting by the window

The day sped by in hide and seek, way too much fun
when one was spied crouched low, draped beside the window

Bustle ebbed in secrets shared, such neat plans we made
while evening's rosy light shown through the window

You and I drew deep breaths, held fast the fleeting day
aware of lights glowing just beyond the window

But time has shifted, the room stills, I see myself
reflected as caught in limbo by the window

Try, Kate, to give back this hush, trade it for past cheer
find a clear view standing solo by the window

Snowbound

Opportunity, a robotic rover, photographed Mars 2004-2018

We talk about the day twenty inches of snow fell
from the sky in a single spate as if that explains

everything even when opportunity died, succumbed
to sand in her eyes after years traveling dusty

roads sending back photos of her adventures tempting
us to peer into those scapes like archeologists sifting

through sand hills piecing together clay shards to tell
the story of opportunity lost and found but it snowed

twenty inches and we found ourselves unable to see
beyond our noses on the very day opportunity died

we heard ice chiming on our windows calling us to brace
our backs against a rock as wind lifted sand from a kneeling

position because spirit died years earlier and what is opportunity
without spirit to see to the other side of a snowbound day

This Silent Night

For Christmas church she wears her good brown dress
and sits alone against an outside wall
as families filter in aglow in red
and green, arranging children, greeting friends,
parading festive spirit, finery
once hers to wear. Accustomed to that warmth,
she prays to move beyond her silent night
to find connection, habit wider spheres.

It seemed so long since she'd been one of them.
Her own, sweet world wrapped in ribbons fast
unraveled like a Christmas spent. Her voice
an empty echo, stillness the reply.
How best to celebrate new life. Amid
the pageantry, she stands and sings alone.

Valentine's Day at the Bistro

At the table next to me a man sits
with the smudge of a cross fixed to his forehead
I came expecting hearts
red paper cutouts
chocolate covered marshmallow goo

What quirk of fate caused the ash of Wednesday
to settle on all-hearts day
Whose voice calls from the great beyond
the teasing trill of a cherub child
or a full-throated throb *with you I am pleased*
or displeased, depending

It's all about love, however we express it
love, that great surprise
the ultimate gooey sacrifice
love, the risk we take
to save ourselves from going it alone

With each passing nod, my fellow diner shares
his smudge of hope, if only we can believe
Amid the lunchtime clatter love waits on us
let the ash settle where it will
Craving Cupid's perfect aim, we pocket our paper hearts

Pulled from a Pocket

I pulled your kiss from my pocket today
the one you waved to me last month saying
put this in your pocket keep it 'til you need it

and I did
need it
today

as an early spring sun warmed my kitchen table
and chickadees sang their sweet-bird song
I reached for you daring to believe in connections

beyond this pandemic still-life to trust
the retreating gloaming will open our days tug
us from our pocket-sized worlds

one day
someday
soon

Have you retrieved my kiss?

An early spring rain is coating my drive

I am icebound

restricted like the trees by this untimely storm
behind me on dusty shelves loom   the books

an entire series wedged corner to corner
their covers muted their spines stiffened with age

twenty-six places tucked high on a shelf
The Badlands Baja   The Great Divide

called by their names to collect month by month
The Ozarks The Bayous   The High Sierra

four decades four houses four times I've shelved them
while pocketing the promise of ever-more time

might I still reach high to retrieve one
release an adventure with the turn of a page

I'll wait   maybe tomorrow   if sun cracks
the ice from those trees leaning against the window

I need brown

I need brown
the nut brown of summer
saturated beach sand shaping to my feet
moist garden soil finger-patted smooth

I need brown
the thrush the catbird chatter of a busy wren
fuchsia flowers popping from my dark brown urn
a weathered garden bench

Enough of winter whiteness
enough of blinding snow
let me rest my eyes on the robin's nest
found twigs knit together to make a home

Monarch

Outside my window, beyond the fence
a monarch clings to the lilac tree
folding, unfolding faceted wings
balanced in morning's savory light.

A monarch clings to the lilac tree
ages ago she scattered her seed
folding, unfolding faceted wings
hope-spun dreams wound in wavering threads.

Ages ago she scattered her seed
trusting to ditches, hedgerows and fields
hope-spun dreams wound in wavering threads
released to adventure on wings edged black.

Trusting to ditches, hedgerows and fields
natural partners bold but adrift
released to adventure on wings edged black
fluttering pulse beats stirring the wind.

Natural partners bold but adrift
folding, unfolding faceted wings
fluttering pulse beats stirring the wind
outside my window, beyond the fence.

Released from a pocket

milkweed fluff floats in still air
drifting above my desk downward
to settle against the unyielding
its plume flattened writing nothing
but a soft breeze stirs from
windows opened and the
seed lifts carrying creation's
weight in its milky web

AT THE DOOR

The traveler

from the seat in front of me fell
toppled like a tree in a windstorm
except inside our bus is very still
each traveler thinking, when is my time
silently bargaining, please let me stand

I think myself home
a first frost sweetens the carrots
I pull them, lay them atop the loamy ground
uprooted, as am I pulled from the familiar
to make my way among strangers
all of us backtracking time

hurry, rain's in the forecast
be quick, lest that shop close
run, the bus is pulling away

I think myself home setting garlic
to take root before the snow

Salubrity

"Live in the sunshine, swim the sea
Drink the wild air's salubrity"

   Merlin's Song by Ralph Waldo Emerson

Breathe   breathe deep   fill your belly   draw air up through
your lungs   let it ripple along the back of your throat   drink
the full-bodied breeze after a warm summer's rain   let it linger
on your tongue   breathe the air crinkling off sun-dried sheets
gulp it in after a run   guard it lest a winter wind steal it away

Here's to our health
a toast to wholesome, vital
air—   salubrity

Three of Cups

The Tarot card, "Three of Cups" represents celebration,
friendship, creativity, and collaboration.

For half a century we have met this way
high school friends sorority sisters home
for the holidays the real draw truth-be-told
our lunch the day after Christmas

At first we didn't think beyond the trendy
holiday sweater that diamond new since last year
we sat—six of us—passing pictures around the table
new baby new house new man new dog sharing
stories honed over twelve months' time

Somewhere along the way we pulled on last year's
sweaters traded pencil skirts for soft-washed jeans
we cried over divorces cancer treatments the errant
child even as we toasted promotions applauded
winning touchdowns celebrated a second marriage

Just three of us now we debate gathering
a countdown of sorts a spin of the wheel the prize
to be next—or last—yet as the day nears we give worry
a pass choosing each to believe she won't be lucky

To the Women of the House

a record number of women serve in the 116th Congress

I still have mine, all of them, tumbled
in a drawer, a wilted rainbow of silk-ribbon
ties in every color, even chartreuse

We knotted them under button-down
collars, narrow links to a life before we
assumed the look, aspired to co-worker
in suits of grey, brown and navy blue

Today, all those decades in a distance,
I watch you swear to uphold in every color
in shawls and skirts and scarves, a bright band,
wearing the workplace as your own.

Winning

Let her win, my mother'd say
even though she never played

My father and I are playing rummy
drawing, discarding, arranging our cards
matching wits

My father likes to win. He holds his cards
close, plays his hand with an eye to the table
strategies learned in the school yard
or maybe the army

My mother wants winning to be a gift
given out of love, a take away but
my father thinks you need to play your hand
snap those cards, winning counts

My mother knows this
even though she's never played

Diary: *March 2020*

The mourning doves do-si-do across the patio

> *I have been walking*
> *walking*
> > *a blister*

a dear couple slightly pudgy through their middles

> *walking*
> > *with care*

they stay close mirroring movements

> *much care*

picking up seeds left in the wake of melting snow

> *alone*
> > *walking*

Humble Days

Awaken to the humble day
unfolding the smooth sheet of time
turn, setting happenstance in play

I used to spurn these freer ways
favoring a tight stretch to time
I've awakened to humble days

Mornings unbound give chance full sway
anything's possible with time
each turn sets happenstance in play

Once I felt lists kept angst at bay
mistook the heavy weight of time
I've awakened to humble days

Left to choose I'm more than okay
with the pace of unbridled time
each turn sets happenstance in play

What to do with this gift   I'd say
ask nothing but to savor time
awaken to the humble day
turn, setting happenstance in play

To Gustava Pedersdatter of Molthrov

Gustava, dear I have been wanting to tell you I found your picture
the one of you and Engebret on your wedding day— sweet it
was with some things Dad saved from Grandma's house they're
both gone now time goes so fast several generations can seem
little more than a year or two how did you do it let your sons
go your first born and his brother then just when you must have
thought enough your baby sailed after them did you think it
was a mother's duty to embrace their lust for adventure tell yourself
they'd come home when their youth was spent what kept you
from crying don't go I know what it's like to give up a son to the
siren call mine to Iraq he came home but for one long second I
didn't recognize the aged man standing at my door did you fear
a loss greater than physical distance you missed their weddings
never held your grandchildren or felt a mother's pride sitting
at their kitchen tables looking out over the lush fields that held
them captive was that a small price to pay to hold your memories
close we're in a pandemic here living out our lives estranged from
family my grandsons growing up without me a hundred miles no
different from an ocean you know what that's like you watched
your youngest return to the homeland to claim his bride only to be
held on the ship while she died of influenza just hours away how
did you hang on to hope we have so much in common you and I
feeling sidelined I suppose but here you are in a picture carried
across an ocean saved for generations— I wanted you to know

On her way

to the library she worries
where to park after dark
recalling rumors of robberies
in her quiet town she chooses the well-lit
but nearly empty lower lot and
holding the half-opened
car door like a shield
slips quickly out clutching
an arm load of books stuffing
keys and mittens in a pocket
she makes her way up the steps and
through the library's revolving door

An hour later hurrying
new books in hand
she retraces her route to stand
knees locked beside her car
patting pockets for her keys
missing her mittens
fearing some stranger will spot her
unguarded in the cold night air when
she sees mittens her mittens
dropped in haste tucked now
between windshield and wiper
by a stranger walking past

My Mother's Will

Her dollars collected wiping chalk dust from cracked blackboards
my mother in endless repetition of two plus two equals what
earned my right to answer   to raise my hand high   to choose
at the end of a long day her wealth measured in friends she brought
home   single mothers ahead of time widows divorced wives who
worked held fast to their bras and Sunday family dinners they
painted my fingernails braided my hair taught me to knit
unraveling time into the corners of their days   I watched them
earn degrees start businesses   all principal players with quiet
resolve they listened   believed my life would equal what I
sought   encouragement steady as the whisper of warm peach jars
sealing on a still August night

Highway 40 feels the same

a roller coaster ride of dips and turns
bringing to mind the eight-year-old I was
unrestrained in the back seat
leaning into the curves, feet braced
stomach lurching, along for the ride
excitement pulsing on worn treads
to Grandmother's house

Half-a-dozen decades later
I'm in control of the wheel
surprised no one's straightened this road
leveled its rolling contours
stretched it along a survey line
until it lay taut as tape
like the measured grades I usually travel

I take my time driving Highway 40
the shoulder's narrow and cruise gives out
braking around too many corners
up ahead Grandma's house waits
shuttered at the edge of a field sprouting willow
I almost miss the turn
holding fast to the feeling that nothing's changed

Skipping

I see her still, a stout figure
thick braids threaded silver, skipping.
One sturdy shoe flung out ahead
the skirt of her house dress swaying
in capricious time as she moved
stiffly up and down the sidewalk

while I stood on the sidewalk's
edge, age five, a forlorn figure
watching my grandmother's feet move.
Try, she called to me. *Try skipping.*
But I, reluctant to be swayed,
stood rooted, not one step ahead.

Her fear I might not move ahead
in school brought us to this sidewalk
with my teacher's note still swaying
in my hand. This note that figured
in our angst. It said skipping
was an essential skill to move

me to first grade, and, so I moved
into line facing straight ahead.
I didn't know my grandmother skipped.
But there she was on the sidewalk
determined I would pass, figuring
intention and her love could sway

me, would draw me to her swaying
rhythm. She beckoned me to move
with her, to imitate her figure.
One smallish shoe nudged out ahead.
I fluttered along the sidewalk
slow to give myself to skipping.

Wondering if I would like to skip
believing I could feel the sway,
I bobbed along the sidewalk.
Drawn by her passion and moved
by her trust, I glided ahead
following my grandma's figure.

Nigh on the age she was then, I can sway
in time, move to the side, walk ahead.
Finally, I have figured out skipping.

Kathleen Serley is a lifelong Wisconsin resident and retired educator. She has a Ph.D from UW-Madison and serves as Mid-Central VP for Wisconsin Fellowship of Poets. Her poems have appeared in *The Solitary Plover*, *Volga River Review*, *Peninsula Pulse*, *Verse Wisconsin*, and *Verse and Vision* where she won the Artists' Choice award.

Made in the USA
Middletown, DE
21 April 2022

64599706R00038